FORWARD/COMMENTARY

The National Institute of Standards and Technology (NIST) is a measurement standards laboratory, and a non-regulatory agency of the United States Department of Commerce. Its mission is to promote innovation and industrial competitiveness. Founded in 1901, as the National Bureau of Standards, NIST was formed with the mandate to provide standard weights and measures, and to serve as the national physical laboratory for the United States. With a world-class measurement and testing laboratory encompassing a wide range of areas of computer science, mathematics, statistics, and systems engineering, NIST's cybersecurity program supports its overall mission to promote U.S. innovation and industrial competitiveness by advancing measurement science, standards, and related technology through research and development in ways that enhance economic security and improve our quality of life.

The need for cybersecurity standards and best practices that address interoperability, usability and privacy has been shown to be critical for the nation. NIST's cybersecurity programs seek to enable greater development and application of practical, innovative security technologies and methodologies that enhance the country's ability to address current and future computer and information security challenges.

The cybersecurity publications produced by NIST cover a wide range of cybersecurity concepts that are carefully designed to work together to produce a holistic approach to cybersecurity primarily for government agencies and constitute the best practices used by industry. This holistic strategy to cybersecurity covers the gamut of security subjects from development of secure encryption standards for communication and storage of information while at rest to how best to recover from a cyber-attack.

Why buy a book you can download for free?

Some are available only in electronic media. Some online docs are missing pages or barely legible.

We at 4th Watch Books are former government employees, so we know how government employees actually use the standards. When a new standard is released, an engineer prints it out, punches holes and puts it in a 3-ring binder. While this is not a big deal for a 5 or 10-page document, many NIST documents are over 100 pages and printing a large document is a time-consuming effort. So, an engineer that's paid $75 an hour is spending hours simply printing out the tools needed to do the job. That's time that could be better spent doing engineering. We publish these documents so engineers can focus on what they were hired to do – engineering. It's much more cost-effective to just order the latest version from Amazon.com

If there is a standard you would like published, let us know. Our web site is Cybah.webplus.net

CyberSecurity Standards Library™

Get a Complete Library of Over 300 Cybersecurity Standards on 1 Convenient DVD!

The **4th Watch CyberSecurity Standards Library** is a DVD disc that puts over 300 current and archived cybersecurity standards from NIST, DOD, DHS, CNSS and NERC at your fingertips! Many of these cybersecurity standards are hard to find and we included the current version and a previous version for many of them. The DVD includes four books written by Luis Ayala: **The Cyber Dictionary, Cybersecurity Standards, Cyber-Security Glossary of Building Hacks and Cyber-Attacks**, and **Cyber-Physical Attack Defenses: Preventing Damage to Buildings and Utilities**.

- ✓ DVD includes many Hard-to-find Cybersecurity Standards - some still in Draft.
- ✓ Docs are organized by source and listed numerically so each standard is easy to locate.
- ✓ The listing of standards on the DVD includes an abstract of the subject, and date issued.
- ✓ PDF format for use on PC, Mac, eReaders, or tablets.
- ✓ No need for WiFi / Internet.
- ✓ Save countless hours of searching and downloading.
- ✓ Carry in a briefcase - terrific for travel.

4th Watch Publishing is releasing the CyberSecurity Standards Library DVD to make it easier for you to access the tools you need to ensure the security of your computer networks and SCADA systems. We also publish many of these standards on demand so you don't need to waste valuable time searching for the latest version of a standard, printing hundreds of pages and punching holes so they can go in a three-ring binder. **Order on Amazon.com**

The DVD works on PC and Mac with the standards in PDF format. To view the CyberSecurity Standards Library on the DVD, a computer with a DVD drive is required. The most current version of your internet browser, at least 2GB of RAM, and current version of Adobe Reader is recommended. (Compatible browsers include Internet Explorer 8+, Mozilla Firefox 4+, Apple Safari 5+, Google Chrome 15+)

NIST Special Publication 800-133

Recommendation for Cryptographic Key Generation

Elaine Barker
Allen Roginsky

http://dx.doi.org/10.6028/NIST.SP.800-133

COMPUTER   SECURITY

National Institute of
Standards and Technology
U.S. Department of Commerce

NIST Special Publication 800-133

Recommendation for Cryptographic Key Generation

Elaine Barker
Allen Roginsky
Computer Security Division
Information Technology Laboratory

http://dx.doi.org/10.6028/NIST.SP.800-133

December 2012

U.S. Department of Commerce
Rebecca Blank, Acting Secretary

National Institute of Standards and Technology
Patrick D. Gallagher, Under Secretary of Commerce for Standards and Technology and Director

National Institute of Standards and Technology Special Publication 800-133
Natl. Inst. Stand. Technol. Spec. Publ. 800-133, 26 pages (December 2012)
http://dx.doi.org/10.6028/NIST.SP.800-133
CODEN: NSPUE2

Comments on this publication may be submitted to:

National Institute of Standards and Technology

Attn: Computer Security Division, Information Technology Laboratory

100 Bureau Drive (Mail Stop 8930) Gaithersburg, MD 20899-8930

Email: SP-800-133_Comments@nist.gov

Reports on Computer Systems Technology

The Information Technology Laboratory (ITL) at the National Institute of Standards and Technology (NIST) promotes the U.S. economy and public welfare by providing technical leadership for the Nation's measurement and standards infrastructure. ITL develops tests, test methods, reference data, proof of concept implementations, and technical analyses to advance the development and productive use of information technology. ITL's responsibilities include the development of management, administrative, technical, and physical standards and guidelines for the cost-effective security and privacy of other than national security-related information in Federal information systems. The Special Publication 800-series reports on ITL's research, guidelines, and outreach efforts in information system security, and its collaborative activities with industry, government, and academic organizations.

Abstract

Cryptography is often used in an information technology security environment to protect data that is sensitive, has a high value, or is vulnerable to unauthorized disclosure or undetected modification during transmission or while in storage. Cryptography relies upon two basic components: an algorithm (or cryptographic methodology) and a cryptographic key. This Recommendation discusses the generation of the keys to be managed and used by the **approved** cryptographic algorithms.

Keywords

asymmetric key; key agreement; key derivation; key generation; key wrapping; key replacement; key transport; key update; private key; public key; symmetric key

Acknowledgements

The National Institute of Standards and Technology (NIST) gratefully acknowledges and appreciates contributions by Rich Davis of the National Security Agency and the public and private sectors whose thoughtful and constructive comments improved the quality and usefulness of this publication.

Table of Contents

Recommendation for Cryptographic Key Generation

1   Introduction

Cryptography is often used in an information technology security environment to protect data that is sensitive, has a high value, or is vulnerable to unauthorized disclosure or undetected modification during transmission or while in storage. Cryptography relies upon two basic components: an algorithm (or cryptographic methodology) and a cryptographic key. The algorithm is a mathematical function, and the key is a parameter used by that function.

The National Institute of Standards and Technology (NIST) has developed a wide variety of Federal Information Processing Standards (FIPS) and NIST Special Publications (SPs) to specify and approve cryptographic algorithms for Federal government use. In addition, guidance has been provided on the management of the cryptographic keys to be used with these **approved** cryptographic algorithms.

This Recommendation discusses the generation of the keys to be used with the **approved** cryptographic algorithms. The keys are either generated using mathematical processing on the output of **approved** Random Bit Generators and possibly other parameters, or generated based upon keys that are generated in this fashion.

2   Authority

This publication has been developed by the National Institute of Standards and Technology (NIST) in furtherance of its statutory responsibilities under the Federal Information Security Management Act (FISMA) of 2002, Public Law 107-347.

NIST is responsible for developing standards and guidelines, including minimum requirements, for providing adequate information security for all agency operations and assets, but such standards and guidelines shall not apply to national security systems.

This Recommendation has been prepared for use by federal agencies. It may be used by non-governmental organizations on a voluntary basis and is not subject to copyright. (Attribution would be appreciated by NIST.)

Nothing in this document should be taken to contradict standards and guidelines made mandatory and binding on federal agencies by the Secretary of Commerce under statutory authority. Nor should these guidelines be interpreted as altering or superseding the existing authorities of the Secretary of Commerce, Director of the OMB, or any other federal official.

Conformance to the requirements in this Recommendation are the responsibility of entities installing, configuring or using applications or protocols that incorporate this Recommendation.

3 Definitions, Acronyms and Symbols

3.1 Definitions

Approved	FIPS-approved and/or NIST-recommended.
Asymmetric key	A cryptographic key used with an asymmetric-key (public-key) algorithm. The key may be a private key or a public key.
Asymmetric-key algorithm	A cryptographic algorithm that uses two related keys, a public key and a private key. The two keys have the property that determining the private key from the public key is computationally infeasible. Also known as a public-key algorithm.
Bit string	An ordered sequence of 0 and 1 bits.
Ciphertext	Data in its encrypted form.
Compromise	The unauthorized disclosure, modification or use of sensitive data (e.g., keying material and other security-related information).
Cryptographic algorithm	A well-defined computational procedure that takes variable inputs, often including a cryptographic key, and produces an output.

Cryptographic key (key)	A parameter used in conjunction with a cryptographic algorithm that determines its operation in such a way that an entity with knowledge of the key can reproduce or reverse the operation, while an entity without knowledge of the key cannot. Examples of cryptographic operations requiring the use of cryptographic keys include: 1. The transformation of plaintext data into ciphertext data, 2. The transformation of ciphertext data into plaintext data, 3. The computation of a digital signature from data, 4. The verification of a digital signature, 5. The computation of an authentication code from data, 6. The verification of an authentication code from data and a received authentication code, 7. The computation of a shared secret that is used to derive keying material. 8. The derivation of additional keying material from a key-derivation key (i.e., a pre-shared key).
Cryptographic module	The set of hardware, software, and/or firmware that implements security functions (including cryptographic algorithms and key generation) and is contained within a cryptographic module boundary. See [FIPS 140].
Cryptographic module boundary	An explicitly defined perimeter (i.e., the set of hardware, software and/or firmware) that establishes the boundary of a cryptographic module. See [FIPS 140].
Cryptoperiod	The time span during which a specific key is authorized for use or in which the keys for a given system or application may remain in effect.
Data integrity	A property possessed by data items that have not been altered in an unauthorized manner since they were created, transmitted or stored.
Decryption	The process of changing ciphertext into plaintext using a cryptographic algorithm and key.

Digital signature	The result of a cryptographic transformation of data that, when properly implemented, provides origin authentication, assurance of data integrity and signatory non-repudiation.
Encryption	The process of changing plaintext into ciphertext using a cryptographic algorithm and key.
Entity	An individual (person), organization, device or process. Used interchangeably with "party".
Entropy	The entropy of a random variable X is a mathematical measure of the expected amount of information provided by an observation of X. As such, entropy is always relative to an observer and his or her knowledge prior to an observation.
Full entropy	For the purposes of this Recommendation, an n-bit string is said to provide full entropy if the string is obtained through a process that is estimated to have at least $(1-\varepsilon)n$ bits of entropy, where $0 \leq \varepsilon \leq 2^{-64}$.
Key	See cryptographic key.
Key agreement	A (pair-wise) key-establishment procedure in which the resultant secret keying material is a function of information contributed by both participants, so that neither party can predetermine the value of the secret keying material independently from the contributions of the other party. Contrast with key transport.
Key-agreement primitive	A primitive algorithm used in a key-agreement scheme specified in [SP 800-56A], or in [SP 800-56B].
Key derivation	1. A process by which one or more keys are derived from a shared secret and other information during a key agreement transaction. 2. A process that derives new keying material from a key (i.e., a key-derivation key) that is currently available.
Key-derivation key	A key used as an input to a key-derivation method to derive other keys. See [SP 800-108].
Key establishment	A procedure that results in secret keying material that is shared among different parties.

Key-generating module	A cryptographic module in which a given key is generated.
Key generation	The process of generating keys for cryptography.
Key pair	A private key and its corresponding public key; a key pair is used with an asymmetric-key (public-key) algorithm.
Key-pair owner	The entity that is authorized to use the private key associated with a public key, whether that entity generated the key pair itself or a trusted party generated the key pair for the entity.
Key transport	A key-establishment procedure whereby one party (the sender) selects a value for the secret keying material and then securely distributes that value to another party (the receiver) using an asymmetric algorithm.
Key update	A procedure in which a new cryptographic key is computed as a function of the (old) cryptographic key that it will replace.
Key wrapping	A method of encrypting and decrypting keys and (possibly) associated data using a symmetric key; both confidentiality and integrity protection are provided.
Module	See Cryptographic module.
Non-repudiation	A service that may be afforded by the appropriate application of a digital signature. Non-repudiation refers to the assurance that the owner of a signature key pair that was capable of generating an existing signature corresponding to certain data cannot convincingly deny having signed the data.
Origin authentication	A process that provides assurance of the origin of information (e.g., by providing assurance of the originator's identity).

Owner	1. For an asymmetric key pair, consisting of a private key and a public key, the owner is the entity that is authorized to use the private key associated with a public key, whether that entity generated the key pair itself or a trusted party generated the key pair for the entity.
	2. For a symmetric key (i.e., a secret key), the entity or entities that are authorized to share and use the key.
Party	See Entity.
Password	A string of characters (letters, numbers and other symbols) that are used to authenticate an identity or to verify access authorization. A passphrase is a special case of a password that is a sequence of words or other text. In this document, the use of the term "password' includes this special case.
Permutation	An ordered (re)arrangement of the elements of a (finite) set; a function that is both a one-to-one and onto mapping of a set to itself.
Plaintext data	In this Recommendation, data that will be encrypted by an encryption algorithm or obtained from ciphertext using a decryption algorithm.
Pre-shared key	A secret key that has been established between the parties who are authorized to use it by means of some secure method (e.g., using a secure manual-distribution process or automated key-establishment scheme).

Private key	A cryptographic key used with an asymmetric-key (public-key) cryptographic algorithm that is not made public and is uniquely associated with an entity that is authorized to use it. In an asymmetric-key cryptosystem, the private key is associated with a public key. Depending on the algorithm that employs the private key, it may be used to: 1. Compute the corresponding public key, 2. Compute a digital signature that may be verified using the corresponding public key, 3. Decrypt data that was encrypted using the corresponding public key, or 4. Compute a key derivation key, which may then be used as an input to a key derivation process.
Public key	A cryptographic key used with an asymmetric-key (public-key) cryptographic algorithm that may be made public and is associated with a private key and an entity that is authorized to use that private key. Depending on the algorithm that employs the public key, it may be used to: 1. Verify a digital signature that is signed by the corresponding private key, 2. Encrypt data that can be decrypted by the corresponding private key, or 3. Compute a piece of shared data (i.e., data that is known only by two or more specific entities).
Public-key algorithm	See Asymmetric-key algorithm.
Random Bit Generator (RBG)	A device or algorithm that outputs bits that are computationally indistinguishable from bits that are independent and unbiased.
Rekey	A procedure in which a new cryptographic key is generated in a manner that is independent of the (old) cryptographic key that it will replace. Contrast with Key update.
Secret key	A cryptographic key used by one or more (authorized) entities in a symmetric-key cryptographic algorithm; the key is not made public.

Secure channel	A path for transferring data between two entities or components that ensures confidentiality, integrity and replay protection, as well as mutual authentication between the entities or components. The secure channel may be provided using cryptographic, physical or procedural methods, or a combination thereof.
Security strength	A number associated with the amount of work (that is, the number of basic operations of some sort) required to break a cryptographic algorithm or system. Security strength is often expressed in bits. If the security strength is S bits, then it is expected that (roughly) 2^S basic operations are required to break the algorithm or system.
Shall	This term is used to indicate a requirement of a Federal Information Processing Standard (FIPS) or a requirement that must be fulfilled to claim conformance to this Recommendation. Note that **shall** may be coupled with **not** to become **shall not**.
Shared secret	A secret value that has been computed using a key-establishment scheme and is used as input to a (single-step) key derivation function or an extraction-then-expansion procedure that derives keying material in a two-step process.
Support a security strength	A term applied to a method (e.g., an RBG, or a key with its associated cryptographic algorithm) that is capable of providing (at a minimum) the security strength required or desired for protecting data.
Symmetric key	See Secret key.
Symmetric-key algorithm	A cryptographic algorithm that uses the same secret key for its operation and, if applicable, for reversing the effects of the operation (e.g., an HMAC key for keyed hashing, or an AES key for encryption and decryption). Also known as a secret-key algorithm.
Target data	The data that is ultimately to be protected (e.g., a key or other sensitive data).

Trusted Party	A party that is trusted by its clients to generate cryptographic keys.

3.2   Acronyms

AES	Advanced Encryption Standard. See [FIPS 197].
CMAC	Cipher-based MAC. See [SP 800-38B].
CTR	Counter mode for a block cipher algorithm. See [SP 800-38A].
DLC	Discrete Logarithm Cryptography.
FIPS	Federal Information Processing Standard.
HMAC	Keyed-Hash Message Authentication Code. See [FIPS 198].
IFC	Integer Factorization Cryptography.
KDF	Key Derivation Function.
MAC	Message Authentication Code.
NIST	National Institute of Standards and Technology.
RBG	Random Bit Generator.
RSA	Rivest-Shamir-Adelman.
SP	Special Publication.

3.3   Symbols

Symbol	Meaning
$\oplus$	Bit-wise exclusive-or. A mathematical operation that is defined as: $$0 \oplus 0 = 0,$$ $$0 \oplus 1 = 1,$$ $$1 \oplus 0 = 1, \text{ and}$$ $$1 \oplus 1 = 0.$$
$\parallel$	Concatenation
$H(x)$	A cryptographic hash function with x as an input.
$T(x, k)$	Truncation of the bit string x to the leftmost k bits of x, where $k \leq$ the length of x in bits.

4   General Discussion

4.1   Keys to Be Generated

This Recommendation addresses the generation of the cryptographic keys used in cryptography. Key generation includes the generation of a key using the output of a random bit generator, the derivation of a key from another key, the derivation of a key from a password, and key agreement performed by two entities using an **approved** key-agreement scheme. All keys **shall** be based directly or indirectly on the output of an **approved** Random Bit Generator (RBG). For the purposes of this Recommendation, keys that are derived during a key-agreement transaction (see [SP 800-56A] and [SP 800-56B]), derived from another key using a key derivation function (see [SP 800-108]) or derived from a password for storage applications (see [SP 800-132]) are considered to be indirectly generated from an RBG, since an ancestor key[1] or random value (e.g., the random value used to generate a key-agreement key pair) was obtained directly from the output of an **approved** RBG.

Two classes of cryptographic algorithms that require cryptographic keys have been **approved** for Federal government use: asymmetric-key algorithms and symmetric-key algorithms. The generation of keys for these algorithm classes is discussed in Sections 6 and 7.

4.2   Where Keys are Generated

Cryptographic keys **shall** be generated within FIPS 140[2]-compliant cryptographic modules [FIPS 140]. For explanatory purposes, consider the cryptographic module in which a key is generated to be the key-generating module. Any random value required by the key-generating module **shall** be generated within that module; that is, the RBG (or portion of the RBG[3]) that generates the random value **shall** be implemented within the FIPS 140 cryptographic module that generates the key. The generated keys **shall** be transported (when necessary) using secure channels and **shall** be used by their associated cryptographic algorithm within FIPS 140-compliant cryptographic modules.

4.3   Supporting a Security Strength

A method (e.g., an RBG, or a key and its associated cryptographic algorithm) *supports a given security strength* if the security strength provided by that method is equal to or greater than the security strength required for protecting the target data; the actual security strength provided can be higher than required.

---

[1] Ancestor key: A key that is used in the generation of another key. For example, an ancestor key for a key generated by a key derivation function would be the key-derivation key used by that key derivation function.

[2] "FIPS 140" without a reference to a particular version is intended to mean the version(s) of the FIPS that are currently being validated (e.g., FIPS 140-2).

[3] The RBG itself might be distributed (e.g., the entropy source may not co-reside with the algorithm that generates the (pseudo) random output). See [FIPS 800-90].

Security strength supported by an RBG: A well-designed RBG supports a given security strength if the amount of entropy (i.e., randomness) available in the RBG is equal to or greater than that security strength. The security strength supported depends on the secrecy of the information designated as the entropy bits and, when used for the generation of keys and other secret values, on the secrecy of the RBG output. For information regarding the security strength that can be supported by **approved** RBGs, see [SP 800-90].

Security strength supported by an algorithm: Discussions of cryptographic algorithms and the security strengths they can support, given certain choices of parameters and/or key lengths, are provided in [SP 800-57-1]. The security strength of a cryptographic algorithm that uses keys of a certain size (i.e., length) is assessed under the assumption that those keys are generated using an **approved** process that provides entropy equal to or greater than the security strength assessed for that algorithm and key size (where both the entropy and the security strength are measured in bits).

Security strength supported by a key: The security strength that can be supported by a key depends on 1) the algorithm with which it is used, 2) the size of the key (see [SP 800-57-1]), 3) the process that generated the key (e.g., the security strength supported by the RBG that was used to generate the key), and 4) how the key was handled (e.g., the security strength available in the method used to transport the key)[4]. The use of such terms as "security strength supported by a key" or "key supports a security strength" assumes that these factors have been taken into account. For example, if an **approved** RBG that supports a security strength of 128 bits has been used to generate a 128-bit key, and if (immediately after generation) the key is used with AES-128 to encrypt target data, then the key may be said to support a security strength of 128 bits in that encryption operation (for as long as the key is kept secret).

5   Using the Output of a Random Bit Generator

Random bit strings required for the generation of cryptographic keys **shall** be obtained from the output of an **approved** Random Bit Generator (RBG); **approved** RBGs are specified in [SP 800-90], [FIPS 186-2], [X9.31] and [X9.62].[5] The RBG **shall** be instantiated at a security strength that supports the security strength required to protect the target data (i.e., the data that will be protected by the generated keys).

The output of an **approved** RBG may be used as specified in this section to obtain either a symmetric key or the random value needed to generate an asymmetric key pair.

Asymmetric key pairs require the use of an **approved** algorithm for their generation.

---

[4] Note that the security strength that can be supported by a key is not solely dependent on its length; for example, even though a 128-bit key is used with AES, an AES operation using that key can only provide 112 bits of security strength if the key was generated using an RBG that supports a security strength of only 112 bits.

[5] [SP 800-90] addresses the issues associated with security strengths, whereas [FIPS 186-2], [X9.31] and [X9.62] do not. Note that in [SP 800-131A], the use of the RBGs specified in [FIPS 186-2], [X9.31] and [X9.62] have been deprecated. Their security strengths may be limited by either the RBG algorithm or the amount of entropy in the RBG seed.

Examples are those included in [FIPS 186-3] for generating DSA, ECDSA and RSA keys. The generation of asymmetric key pairs from a random value is discussed in Section 6.

Methods for the generation of symmetric keys are discussed in Section 7.

Let K be either a symmetric key or the random value to be used as input to an **approved** asymmetric-key pair generation algorithm. K **shall** be a bit string value of the following form:

$$K = U \oplus V, \tag{1}$$

where

- U is a bit string of the desired length that is obtained as the output of an **approved** Random Bit Generator (RBG) that is capable of supporting the desired security strength required to protect the target data,

- V is a bit string of the same length as U, and

- The value of V is determined in a manner that is independent of the value of U (and vice-versa).

The algorithm with which K will be used, and the security strength that this usage is intended to support will determine the required bit length and/or the minimum security strength that this process must provide. Since there are no restrictions on the selection of V (other than its length and its independence from U), a conservative approach necessitates an assumption that the process used to select U provides most (if not all) of the required entropy.

The independence requirement on U and V is interpreted in a computational and a statistical sense; that is, the computation of U does not depend on V, the computation of V does not depend on U, and knowing one of the values (U or V) must yield no information that can be used to gain insight into the other value. Assuming that U is the output of an **approved** RBG, the following are examples of independently selected V values:

1. V is a constant (selected independently from the value of U). (Note, that if V is a string of binary zeroes, then $K = U$, i.e., the output of an **approved** RBG.)

2. V is a key obtained using an **approved** key-derivation method from a key-derivation key and other input that is independent of U; see SP 800-108.

3. V is a key that was independently generated in another cryptographic module. V was protected using an **approved** key-wrapping algorithm or transported using an **approved** key transport scheme during subsequent transport. Upon receipt, the protection on V is removed within the key-generating module that generated U before combining V with U.

4. V is produced by hashing another bit string (V') using an **approved** hash function and (if necessary) truncating the result to the appropriate length before combining it with U. That is, $V = \mathrm{T}(\mathrm{H}(V'), k)$ where $\mathrm{T}(x, k)$ denotes the truncation of bit string x to its k leftmost bits, and k is the length of U. The bit string V' may be a)

a constant; b) a key derived from a shared secret during an **approved** key-agreement scheme between the key-generating module and another cryptographic module; or c) a key that was i) independently generated by another module, ii) sent using an **approved** key wrapping algorithm or transported using an **approved** key transport scheme, and iii) upon receipt, the protection on the key was removed.

6 Generation of Key Pairs for Asymmetric-Key Algorithms

Asymmetric-key algorithms, also known as public-key algorithms, require the use of asymmetric key pairs, consisting of a private key and a corresponding public key. The key to be used for each operation depends on the cryptographic process being performed (e.g., digital-signature generation or verification). Each public/private key pair is associated with only one entity; this entity is known as the key-pair owner. The public key may be known by anyone, whereas the private key must be known and used only by the key-pair owner. Key pairs **shall** be generated by:

- The key-pair owner, or

- A Trusted Party that provides the key pair to the owner in a secure manner. The Trusted Party must be trusted by all parties that use the public key.

6.1 Key Pairs for Digital Signature Schemes

Digital signatures are generated on data to provide origin authentication, assurance of data integrity or signatory non-repudiation. Digital signatures are generated by a signer using a private key, and verified by a receiver using a public key. The generation of key pairs for digital signature applications is addressed in [FIPS 186-3] for the DSA, RSA and ECDSA digital signature algorithms.

A value of K, computed as shown in Section 5, **shall** be used to provide the random value needed to generate a key pair for DSA, ECDSA or RSA as specified in [FIPS 186-3]. The maximum security strength that can be supported by these algorithms and the key lengths used by these algorithms are provided in [SP 800-57-1].

For example, [SP 800-57-1] states that a DSA key pair with a public-key length of 2048 bits and a private-key length of 224 bits can support (at most) a security strength of 112 bits. [FIPS 186-3] specifies that for such DSA key pairs, the random value used to determine a private key must be obtained using an RBG that supports a security strength of 112 bits. Using the method in Section 5, a random value K that is to be used for the generation of the key pair is determined by U (a value of an appropriate bit length obtained from an RBG that supports a security strength of at least 112 bits) and V (which could be zero). The value K is then used to determine the DSA key pair, as specified in [FIPS 186-3].

6.2 Key Pairs for Key Establishment

Key establishment includes both key agreement and key transport. Key agreement is a method of key establishment in which the resultant secret keying material is a function of information contributed by the participants, so that no party can predetermine the value of the keying material independent of any other party's contribution. For key-transport, one party (the sender) selects a value for the secret keying material and then securely distributes that value to another party (the receiver).

Approved methods for generating the (asymmetric) key pairs used by **approved** key-establishment schemes between two parties are specified in [SP 800-56A] (for schemes that use finite-field or elliptic-curve cryptography) and in [SP 800-56B] (for schemes that use integer-factorization cryptography, e.g., RSA).

A value of K, computed as shown in Section 5, **shall** be used to provide the random value[6] needed to generate key pairs for the finite field or elliptic curve schemes in [SP 800-56A], or to generate a key pair for the integer-factorization schemes specified in [SP 800-56B]. The maximum security strength that can be supported by the **approved** key-establishment schemes and the key sizes used by these schemes is provided in [SP 800-57-1].

6.3   Distributing the Key Pairs

A general discussion of the distribution of asymmetric key pairs is provided in [SP 800-57-1].

The private key **shall** be kept secret. It **shall** either be generated 1) within the key-pair owner's cryptographic module (i.e., the key-pair owner's key-generating module), or 2) within the cryptographic module of an entity trusted by the key-pair owner and any relying party not to misuse the private key or reveal it to other entities (i.e., generated within the key-generating module of a Trusted Party, and securely transferred to the key-pair owner's cryptographic module).

If a private key is ever output from a cryptographic module, the key **shall** be output and transferred in a form and manner that provides appropriate assurance[7] of its confidentiality and integrity. The protection **shall** provide appropriate assurance that only the key-pair owner and/or the party that generated the key pair will be able to determine the value of the plaintext private key (e.g., the confidentiality and integrity protection for the private key uses a cryptographic mechanism that is at least as strong as the (maximum) security strength that must be supported by the asymmetric algorithm that will use the private key).

The public key of a key pair may be made public. However, it **shall** be distributed and verified in a manner that assures its integrity and association with the key-pair owner (e.g., using a X.509 certificate that provides a level of cryptographic protection that is at least as strong as the security strength associated with the key pair).

---

[6] Note that in Section 5, if V is all zeroes, then K (the random value) is the output of an RBG.

[7] The term "provide appropriate assurance" is used to allow various methods for the input and output of critical security parameters to/from the different security levels that may be implemented for a cryptographic module (see [FIPS 140] and Section 7.8 of [ImpGuide]).

7   Generation of Keys for Symmetric-Key Algorithms

Symmetric-key algorithms use the same (secret) key to both apply cryptographic protection to information[8] and to remove or verify the protection[9]. Keys used with symmetric-key algorithms must be known by only the entities authorized to apply, remove or verify the protection, and are commonly known as secret keys. A secret key is often known by multiple entities that are said to share or own the secret key, although it is not uncommon for a key to be generated, owned and used by a single entity (e.g., for secure storage). A secret key **shall** be generated by:

- One or more of the entities that will share the key, or

- A Trusted Party that provides the key to the intended sharing entities in a secure manner. The Trusted Party must be trusted by all entities that will share the key not to disclose the key to unauthorized parties or otherwise misuse the key.

A symmetric key K could be used, for example, to:

- Encrypt and decrypt data in an appropriate mode (e.g., using AES in the CTR mode as specified in [FIPS 197] and SP [800-38A]),

- Generate Message Authentication Codes (e.g., using AES in the CMAC mode, as specified in [FIPS 197] and [SP 800-38B], or HMAC, as specified in [FIPS 198], or

- Derive additional keys using a key derivation function specified in [SP 800-108], where K is the pre-shared key that is used as the key-derivation key.

7.1   The "Direct Generation" of Symmetric Keys

Symmetric keys that are to be directly generated from the output of an RBG **shall** be generated as specified in Section 5, where K is the desired key. The length of the key to be generated is determined by the algorithm with which it will be used and the desired security strength to be provided; see [SP 800-57-1] for discussions on key lengths and the (maximum) security strengths supported by symmetric-key algorithms.

7.2   Distributing the Generated Symmetric Key

The symmetric key generated within the key-generating module often needs to be shared with one or more other entities that have their own cryptographic modules. The key may be distributed manually, or using an **approved** key transport or key wrapping method (see [SP 800-56A], [SP 800-56B] and [SP 800-38F]). See [SP 800-57-1] for further discussion. The method used for key transport or key wrapping **shall** support the desired security strength needed to protect the target data (i.e., the data to be protected using the

---

[8] For example, transform plaintext data into ciphertext data using an encryption operation or compute a message authentication code (MAC).

[9] For example, remove the protection by transforming the ciphertext data back to the original plaintext data using a decryption operation, or verify the protection by computing a message authentication code and comparing the newly computed MAC with a received MAC)

symmetric key). The requirements for outputting a key from a cryptographic module are discussed in [FIPS 140].

7.3 Symmetric Keys Generated Using Key-Agreement Schemes

When an **approved** key-agreement scheme is available within an entity's key-generating module, a symmetric key may be established with another entity that has the same capability; this process results in a symmetric key that is shared between the two entities participating in the key-agreement transaction; further distribution of this symmetric key is not required between the two entities.

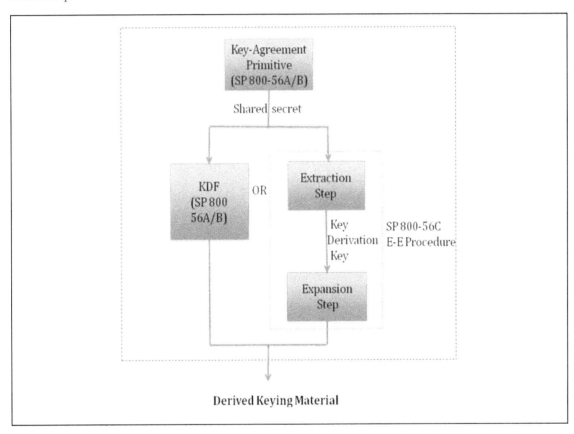

Figure 1: Key-agreement Process per SP 800-56A, B and C

Figure 1 depicts a typical key-agreement process. Asymmetric key-agreement keys are used with a key-agreement primitive to generate a shared secret. The shared secret is provided to a key-derivation method (e.g., a single-step key derivation function or an extraction-then-expansion (E-E) procedure) to derive keying material. [SP 800-56A] specifies **approved** key-agreement methods based on DLC; [SP 800-56B] includes specifications for **approved** key-agreement methods based on IFC. **Approved** single-step key derivation functions are specified in [SP 800-56A] and [SP 800-56B]; **approved** extraction-then-expansion procedures are specified in [SP 800-56C] and may be used by the key-agreement schemes, as specified in [SP 800-56A].

The key-agreement schemes used by many widely used internet security protocols do not fully comply with [SP 800-56A] and [SP 800-56B]. For example, the key-derivation method used to derive keying material from the shared secret may be different. [SP 800-135] discusses some of these protocols, **conditionally approves** the use of the key derivation functions employed by those protocols, and specifies requirements for that **approved** use.

The maximum security strength that can be supported by a key derived in this manner is dependent on 1) the security strength supported by the asymmetric key pairs (as used during key establishment), 2) the key-derivation method used, 3) the length of the derived key and 4) the algorithm with which the derived key will be used. See [SP 800-57-1] for items 1, 3 and 4. For item 2, see [SP 800-56A], [SP 800-56B] and [SP 800-56C] when the key-derivation method specified therein is used; no statement is made at this time concerning the security strengths that may be supported by a key derived using the methods specified in [SP 800-135].

7.4   Symmetric Keys Derived From a Pre-shared Key

Symmetric keys are often derived using a key derivation function (KDF) and a pre-shared key known as a key-derivation key. The pre-shared key may have been:

- Generated from an **approved** RBG (see Section 5) and distributed as specified in Section 7.2, if required,

- Agreed upon using a key-agreement scheme (see Section 7.3), or

- Derived using a KDF and a (different) pre-shared key as specified in [SP 800-108].

Approved methods are provided in [SP 800-108], which specifies **approved** KDFs for deriving keys from a pre-shared key (i.e., a key-derivation key). The KDFs are based on HMAC [FIPS 198] and CMAC [SP 800-38B].

If the derived keys need to be distributed to other entities, this may be accomplished as discussed in Section 7.2.

In addition to the symmetric algorithm with which a derived key will be used, the security strength that can be supported by the derived key depends on the security strength supported by the key-derivation key and the KDF method used (see [SP 800-57-1] for the maximum security strength that can be supported by HMAC and CMAC, and [SP 800-107] for further discussions about the security strength of HMAC).

7.5   Symmetric Keys Derived From Passwords

In a number of popular applications, keys are generated from passwords. This is a questionable practice, as the passwords usually contain very little entropy (i.e., randomness), and are, therefore, easily guessed. However, **approved** methods for deriving keys from passwords for storage applications are provided in [SP 800-132]. For these applications, users are strongly advised to select passwords with a very large amount of entropy.

When a key is generated from a password, the entropy provided (and thus, the maximum security strength that can be supported by the generated key) **shall** be considered to be zero unless the password is generated using an **approved** RBG. In this case, the security strength that can be supported by the password (*password_strength*) is no greater than the minimum of the security strength supported by the RBG (*RBG_strength*) and the actual number of bits of RBG output (*RBG_outlen*) used in the password. That is, *password_strength* $\leq$ min(*RBG_strength*, *RBG_outlen*).

7.6 Symmetric Keys Produced by Combining Multiple Keys and Other Data

When symmetric keys $K_1, \ldots, K_n$ are generated and/or established independently, they may be combined within a key-generating module to form a key K. Other items of data ($V_1, \ldots, V_m$) that are independent of these keys can also be combined with the K_i to form K, under the conditions specified below. Note that, while the K_i values are required to be secret, the V_i values need not be kept secret.

The independent generation/establishment of the component keys $K_1, \ldots, K_n$ is interpreted in a computational and a statistical sense; that is, the computation of any particular K_i value does not depend on any one or more of the other K_i values, and it is not feasible to use knowledge of any proper subset of the K_i values to obtain any information about the remaining K_i values.

The independence of the component keys from the other items of data is also interpreted in a computational and a statistical sense. This means that the computation of the K_i values does not depend on any of the V_j values, the computation of the V_j values does not depend on any of the K_i values, and knowledge of the V_j values yields no information that can feasibly be used to gain insight into the K_i values. In cases where some (or all) of the V_j values are secret, and the rest of the V_j values (if any) are public, "independence" also means that knowledge of the K_i values and public V_j values yields no information that can feasibly be used to gain insight into the secret V_j values.

The component symmetric keys $K_1, \ldots, K_n$ **shall** be generated and/or established independently using **approved** methods[10]. The other items of data (i.e., $V_1, \ldots, V_m$) may be generated or obtained using any method that ensures their independence from those keys.

The **approved** methods for combining these symmetric keys (and other items of data) are:

1. Concatenating two or more keys, i.e., $K = K_1 \| \ldots \| K_n$. The sum of the bit lengths of the n component keys **shall** be equal to the required bit length of K.

2. Exclusive-Oring one or more symmetric keys, i.e., $K = K_1 \oplus \ldots \oplus K_n$. The length of each component key (K_i) **shall** be equal to the length required for K.

---

[10] See Sections 7.1, 7.3, 7.4 and 7.5.

3. Exclusive-Oring one or more symmetric keys and one or more other items of data, i.e., $K = K_1 \oplus \ldots \oplus K_n \oplus V_1 \oplus \ldots \oplus V_m$. The length of each component key (K_i) and each item of data (V_i) **shall** be equal to the length required for K.

Each K_i used in one of the three methods above **shall** be kept secret, **shall** be considered a key-derivation key, and **shall not** be used for any purpose other than the computation of a specific symmetric key K (i.e., a given K_i **shall not** be used to generate more than one key).

7.7 Replacement of Symmetric Keys

Sometimes, a symmetric key may need to be replaced. This may be due to a compromise of the key or the end of the key's cryptoperiod (see [SP 800-57-1]). Replacement may be accomplished by a rekeying process or by a key-update process. Rekeying is the replacement of a key with a new key that is generated in a manner that is entirely independent of the value of the old key (i.e., knowledge of the old key provides no knowledge of the value of the replaced key and vice versa). In a key-update process, the new key is usually related in some way to the old key that it replaces.

Compromised keys **shall** only be rekeyed, rather than updated. When a compromised key is replaced, the new key **shall** be generated in a manner that provides assurance of its independence from the compromised key. The new key may be generated using any method in Section 7 with the following restrictions:

1. The method used **shall** provide assurance that there is no feasibly detectable relationship between the new key and the compromised key. To that end, the new key **shall not** be derived or updated using the compromised key.

2. If the compromised key was generated in a manner that depended (in whole or in part) on a password (see Sections 7.5 and 7.6), then that password **shall** be changed prior to the generation of any new key; in particular, the new key(s) **shall** be generated in a manner that is independent of the old password value.

If an uncompromised symmetric key is to be replaced, it **shall** be replaced using any method in Section 7 that supports the required amount of security strength. However, if the key to be replaced was generated in a manner that depended (in whole or in part) on a password (see Sections 7.5 and 7.6), that password **shall** be changed prior to the generation of the new key.

Appendix A: References

[FIPS 140]   FIPS 140-2, Security Requirements for Cryptographic Modules, May 2001, available at http://csrc.nist.gov/publications/PubsFIPS.html.

[FIPS 180]   FIPS 180-4, Secure Hash Standard, March 2012.

[FIPS 186-2]   Digital Signature Standard, January 2000.

[FIPS 186-3]   FIPS 186-3, Digital Signature Standard, June 2009.

[FIPS 197]   Advanced Encryption Standard (AES), November 2001.

[FIPS 198]   FIPS 198-1, Keyed-Hash Message Authentication Code (HMAC), July 2008.

[SP 800-38A]   Recommendation for Block Cipher Modes of Operation - Methods and Techniques, December 2001.

[SP 800-38B]   SP 800-38B, Recommendation for Block Cipher Modes of Operation: The CMAC Mode for Authentication, May 2005.

[SP 800-38F]   DRAFT Recommendation for Block Cipher Modes of Operation: Methods for Key Wrapping, August 2011 (Draft).

[SP 800-56A]   SP 800-56A, Recommendation for Pair-Wise Key Establishment Schemes Using Discrete Logarithm Cryptography, March 2007.

[SP 800-56B]   SP 800-56B, Recommendation for Pair-Wise Key Establishment Using Integer Factorization Cryptography, August 2009.

[SP 800-56C]   SP 800-56C, Recommendation for Key Derivation through Extraction-then-Expansion, November 2011.

[SP 800-57-1] SP 800-57, Part 1, Recommendation for Key Management: General, July 2012.

[SP 800-67]   Recommendation for the Triple Data Encryption Algorithm (TDEA) Block Cipher, January 2012.

[SP 800-90]   SP 800-90A, Recommendation for Random Number Generation Using Deterministic Random Bit Generators, January 2012.

               Draft SP 800-90B, Recommendation for the Validation of Entropy Sources for Random Bit Generation, September 5, 2012.

               Draft SP 800-90C, Recommendation for Random Bit Generator (RBG) Constructions, September 5, 2012.

[SP 800-108]   SP 800-108, Recommendation for Key Derivation Using Pseudorandom Functions (Revised), October 2009.

[SP 800-131A] Recommendation for the Transitioning of Cryptographic Algorithms and Key Lengths, January 2011.

[SP 800-132] SP 800-132, Recommendation for Password-Based Key Derivation, Part 1: Storage Applications, December 2010.

[SP 800-135] SP 800-135, Recommendation for Existing Application-Specific Key Derivation Functions, December 2010.

[ImpGuide] Implementation Guidance for FIPS PUB 140-2 and the Cryptographic Module Validation Program, available at http://csrc.nist.gov/groups/STM/cmvp/standards.html.

[X9.31] American National Standard (ANS) X9.31-1998, Digital Signatures Using Reversible Public Key Cryptography for the Financial Services Industry (rDSA), Withdrawn, but available from X9.org.

[X9.62] American National Standard X9.62-2005, Public Key Cryptography for the Financial Services Industry: The Elliptic Curve Digital Signature Algorithm (ECDSA), available at x9.org.

www.ingramcontent.com/pod-product-compliance
Lightning Source LLC
La Vergne TN
LVHW060149070326
832902LV00018B/3030